T0031533

Fantastic Kids

Care for Animals

Kristy Stark, M.A.Ed.

Publishing Credits

Rachelle Cracchiolo, M.S.Ed., *Publisher*
Conni Medina, M.A.Ed., *Managing Editor*
Nika Fabienke, Ed.D., *Series Developer*
June Kikuchi, *Content Director*
John Leach, *Assistant Editor*
Kevin Pham, *Graphic Designer*

TIME For Kids and the TIME For Kids logo are registered trademarks of TIME Inc.
Used under license.

Image Credits: All images from iStock and/or Shutterstock.

Library of Congress Cataloging-in-Publication Data

Names: Stark, Kristy, author.
Title: Fantastic kids : care for animals / Kristy Stark, M.A.Ed.
Description: Huntington Beach, CA : Teacher Created Materials, [2018] |
   Audience: K to Grade 3.
Identifiers: LCCN 2017030000 (print) | LCCN 2017031773 (ebook) | ISBN
   9781425853266 (eBook) | ISBN 9781425849528 (pbk.)
Subjects: LCSH: Pets--Juvenile literature.
Classification: LCC SF413 (ebook) | LCC SF413 .S73 2018 (print) | DDC
   636.088/7--dc23
LC record available at https://lccn.loc.gov/2017030000

Teacher Created Materials

5301 Oceanus Drive
Huntington Beach, CA 92649-1030
http://www.tcmpub.com

ISBN 978-1-4258-4952-8

© 2018 Teacher Created Materials, Inc.

Take care of living things.

Lynn has a dog.

She takes care
of it.

Anne has a fish.

She takes care
of it.

Chris has a cat.

He takes care
of it.

Joe has a horse.

He takes care
of it.

You can make an
animal happy.